DISARRANGEMENTS IN THE

FOURTH GOSPEL

DISARRANGEMENTS IN THE
FOURTH GOSPEL

BY

F. WARBURTON LEWIS, B.A.
MANSFIELD COLLEGE, OXFORD.
TRINITY COLLEGE, CAMBRIDGE.

Cambridge:
at the University Press
1910

CAMBRIDGE
UNIVERSITY PRESS

University Printing House, Cambridge CB2 8BS, United Kingdom

Published in the United States of America by Cambridge University Press, New York

Cambridge University Press is part of the University of Cambridge.

It furthers the University's mission by disseminating knowledge in the pursuit of
education, learning and research at the highest international levels of excellence.

www.cambridge.org
Information on this title: www.cambridge.org/9781107416239

© Cambridge University Press 1910

First published 1910
First paperback edition 2014

A catalogue record for this publication is available from the British Library

ISBN 978-1-107-41623-9 Paperback

CONTENTS

	PAGES
The Thesis	1
VI	3
V and VII	6
Chronology of above	10
Spitta	14
VII 53–VIII 11	16
VIII 12–20	17
21–59	22
Note on XII	24
II and III	25
Chronology of above	31
XIII–XVII	35
Conclusion	51

DISARRANGEMENTS IN THE
FOURTH GOSPEL

IT is generally understood among students of the New Testament that the text of the Fourth Gospel has suffered by disarrangement, but surprisingly little notice has been given to the subject. One explores wide reaches of the Johannine literature only to find no reference to the subject.

What has been written directly on the subject at all usefully will be found referred to, for the greater part, in the pages following. There is no reference to Wellhausen's suggestions in his recent *Erweiterungen* only because he has not followed fruitful lines of investigation.

This Essay is really a sequel to the relevant section of Spitta's work[1] referred to throughout. But even Spitta has only dealt with a part of the subject. I have gone over his ground independently, and added what must be termed newly discovered passages that have been displaced from their original position. It is only such passages that have place in the present investigation. For this reason there is no notice of Spitta's discussion of the alleged disorder in XVIII 12–28, or of any such supposed disorder in the Prologue. Our subject is that of passages now found in positions which they did not originally occupy, or which they were not meant to occupy by the writer. This alternative it is necessary to state

---

[1] *Zur Geschichte und Litteratur des Urchristenthums*, von Friedrich Spitta, pp. 156—204.

for completeness' sake, for it is not possible to prove whether the disorder arose in the disruption of some early copy of the Gospel after it had been completed, or whether it was caused by original ill-arrangement of the writer's material. It will conduce to clearness, if we take the former as a working hypothesis.

Then an attempt is made to re-construct the original order of the Gospel, and to show the bearing of the re-arrangement on the subject of the chronology of the Life of Christ, as well as upon, in each case, the exegesis of the passages and their contexts.

The name "John" is used without prejudice to the question of authorship. Our investigation is really preliminary to all other investigations except those of a still more purely textual character.

Finally, I would take Spitta's words for my own, when, after speaking of attempts to re-arrange the Prologue as springing from "the idea that the train of thought in question did not agree with that which the commentator expected to find," he adds on his own behalf:—"My hope of a friendly reception of this hypothesis rests mainly on this, that the motive that leads to it is in no way concerned with the niceties of a commentator in reviewing S. John's train of thought, but on peculiarities in the text which strike the eye of a layman. I hope also to be able to show that a knowledge of the original connection is not worthless in considering these extracts, nor worthless for the whole Gospel."

It may be added that of the passages to be examined, Spitta only deals with XIII–XVII, VII 15–24 and the *pericope adulterae*.

VI.

We begin with the position of VI.

It is not surprising to find that the present position of this chapter has for long been a subject of question and discussion, though it is surprising that the needed and inevitable re-arrangement has not been seriously taken into consideration in the study of the chronology of the Life of Christ.

As long ago as the fourteenth century a re-arrangement in the order of the chapters was suggested by Ludolphus de Saxonia in his *Vita Christi Evangelicis et scriptoribus orthodoxis excerpta*[1]. But even to the present day the obvious misplacement has not been duly recognised in its bearing on such a question, e.g., as that of the "feast" mentioned in V.

The position is as follows :—

IV brings Jesus to Galilee (43–54) and ends with words that lead us to expect a period of ministry in Galilee : "having come out of Judaea into Galilee." But

V inconsequently brings Him back to Jerusalem, and leaves Him there.   Whereas

[1] J. P. Norris, *Journal of Philology* (1871), vol. III, pp. 107–112.

VI opens in Galilee. And not only is Jesus in Galilee instead of being in Jerusalem where V left Him, but we find Him in the *first* verse crossing from one side of the Lake of Galilee to the other—i.e. VI 1 actually presupposes that He is in Galilee, whereas the now preceding chapter only speaks of Him as being in Jerusalem.

Again: VII opens with a statement that Jesus would not walk any longer in Judaea, and therefore resorted to Galilee, where, according to the preceding chapter, He already was. This chapter, therefore, is likė Chapter VI in presupposing in its opening words precisely the situation that is not found in the narrative immediately foregoing.

All this confusion is ended by the simple transposition of V and VI. This gives the natural order of the chapters

IV

VI

V

VII

Christ's return to Galilee (IV 43) is followed by what IV 54 leads us to expect, a period of work in Galilee (VI 1–2) culminating in the crisis of the Galilean ministry (4–66).

And the breach with His disciples ("many" VI 66) and with the people (VI passim) is followed by withdrawal, and ultimately by a period of ministry in Jerusalem (V and VII).

Moreover we can by this re-arrangement, if we desire, give the natural interpretation to IV 35 ("Yet four months, and then cometh harvest"): Jesus returned in December, and His resumed ministry in Galilee (45 ff.) culminated in the dramatic and critical crisis of VI four months later at the Passover of A.D. 28.

And we are now free to regard the "feast" of V as the subsequent Pentecost, if we find that this accords with other facts and considerations.

The full chronological import of the re-arrangement must however be left to a subsequent stage of the investigation.

The result thus reached is still more strongly confirmed by the initial facts of the next section.

V and VII.

(i) By the transposition of V and VI thus made, V and VII are brought into conjunction.

Investigation shows that this conjunction is confirmed by internal evidence, some such interval as that between the Feasts of Pentecost and Tabernacles being the utmost that can be supposed to have elapsed in view of the facts that VII takes up the situation of V and carries it on, and that the attitude of the " Jews" to Christ revealed in VII is the sequel of that in V.

More particularly :—

VII 1 accounts for Christ's departure from Judaea by saying that "the Jews were seeking to *kill* Him."

This exactly answers to the situation of V, for in V 16 persecution breaks out, and in ver. 18 we have the first record of the design to kill Him.

If we may anticipate a result which we shall reach in a later part of this section, V really has its conclusion in a paragraph now misplaced, viz. VII 15–24, and though the present argument does not depend upon this replacement, it is better to take it into consideration in tracing the development of the situation.

We thus have clearly before us the course of events recorded in V and VII: the outbreak of persecution (V 16) developes into the settled policy of violence (18), and this intention to kill becomes known to Jesus, and publicly spoken of (VII 19, 20). With this knowledge of His life being in danger, Jesus leaves Judaea and returns to Galilee (VII 1). Acting in accordance therewith, He in due time, on the advent of the Feast of Tabernacles, exercises great circumspection in going up to Jerusalem, avoiding the accustomed way and time, and appearing in the city only after His enemies have ceased to keep watch for Him (VII 2–14). Once in the midst of the people, He is comparatively safe. But the development of the situation that we are tracing is immediately confirmed and carried forward in the next verse (omitting 15–24)—i.e. in VII 25 : His advent in the Temple (14) is at once greeted by the amazed question : " Is not this He whom they are seeking to kill ? "

This clear development of events, proceeding, as it does, through the remaining part of VII, and carried on, as we shall see, into the connected chapter VIII, is precisely the confirmation we need of this re-arrangement of the chapters.

On the other hand it is completely broken up by the present insertion of VI between V and VII, an insertion entailing an interval of many months, even of eighteen months, if the " feast " of V is taken to be a Passover.

(ii) The paragraph VII 15–24, referred to above in anticipation, is out of place where it is now found, and entirely in place at the end of V.

This is taken from F. Spitta's *Zur Geschichte und Litteratur des Urchristenthums*, 199 ff., and is accepted by E. D. Burton[1], by J. Moffat[2], and by others, among them being Wendt[3].

Investigation again leads us to see the naturalness of the new order.

In the first place, the consecutiveness of VII in itself is greatly enhanced by the removal of a wedge of foreign matter : when verses 15–24 are deleted, verse 25 exactly follows upon verses 1–14. There is no need to labour this point.

In the second place, VII 15–24 is obviously part of V. Reading the narrative thus: V + VII 15–24, we see that :—

(1) VII 15 ("How knoweth this man letters, having never learned ?") exactly follows and answers to V 47, with its reference to the "writings of Moses," and to the knowledge of them displayed (39, 45–47).

(2) VII 16–19[a] takes up and completes the argument of V 30–47 : "My teaching is not Mine, but His that sent Me" (16) takes up V 30 f. as that in its turn had taken up V 19; VII 17 as surely gathers up the contention of V 37–40, just as the verses following in each chapter, V 18 and VII 41–44, answer to each other in their treatment of the subject of true and false glory ; and the immediate parallel is closed by the references to Moses and his law in VII 19[a] and V 45–47. Thus the whole of V 30–47 is taken up and brought to an argumentative climax in VII 16–19[a].

---

[1] *Biblical World*, vol. XIII, p. 30.

[2] *Historical New Testament*, ad loc. The re-arrangement is taken into his translation.

[3] *The Gospel according to St John* (pp. 85 ff., Eng. trans.).

(3) Ver. 19^b ("Why are ye seeking to kill Me?") standing where it now does, is in the air, there being nothing in the preceding narrative since the arrival of Jesus in Jerusalem (14) to which it can refer. The question is in the present tense, and does not refer to an action of months ago. Moreover it is "impossible" just before VII 25: "Is not this He whom they are seeking to kill?"—a question entirely out of place immediately after Christ's open question in ver. 19^b quoted above, and equally so after ver. 13. But with our paragraph replaced at the end of V, the question, which is in the present tense, naturally refers to ver. 18 of that chapter, "the Jews sought the more to kill Him." We see that V 18 and VII 19^b are contemporaneous.

(4) Even more obvious are the references in VII 21 ("I did one work") and ver. 23 ("I made a man every whit whole on the Sabbath") to the healing of the blind man on the Sabbath in V 2–9, and to the scandal which arose subsequently.

(5) And VII 24 ("Judge not according to appearance, but judge righteous judgment") forms the conclusion of the entire paragraph (V 30–47 + VII 15–24), and echoes the words of the opening sentence: "as I hear, I judge; and My judgment is righteous" (V 30).

It is therefore clear that we have not here, in V 19–47 and VII 15–24, two passages separated by five months, at least, one of them spoken at the Feast of Pentecost[1], the other at the Feast of Tabernacles,

---

[1] Under the arrangement of chapters as they now stand in the New Testament, with VI between V and VII, the gap was of course wider,

and to diverse audiences. The references we have examined and the completion of the argument of V in the other passages demand that we regard VII 15–24 as the conclusion of the fifth chapter.

I regard as unfounded the suggestion that in VII verses 45–52 should precede 37–44 on the ground that 45 should fall on the same day as 32. It is not necessary to regard 32 as pointing to the intention of immediate arrest, but only to an arrest on some opportune occasion during the feast. So the report of the officers that no such opportunity seemed to present itself is not in place until after the end of the feast, where indeed we now find it, rightly following " the last day " (37 f.).

So far then our re-arrangement of chapters is :—

IV
VI
V + VII 15–24
VII 1–14, 25–52

These chapters are not yet complete, but, without anticipating, we may now garner our first result in the field of the chronology of the Gospels.

We have these dates clearly before us :—

VI	.	.	.	Passover A.D. 28.
				‖ Mk. VI 30 f., Lk. IX 10 f.
V + VII 15–24	.	Pentecost
VII 1–14, 25–52	Tabernacles
XII–XIX .	.	Passover A.D. 29.

at its narrowest seven months in extent, the latest possible date for V being the Feast of Purim ; at its widest, eighteen months.

Here lies the outline of the last year of the ministry of Jesus. And, without seeking them for harmonistic purposes, we gain the following results:—

(1) The vexed problem of the "feast" of V is solved. It falls naturally at Pentecost, one of the chief feasts of the year, seven weeks after the time of the Passover of VI 4.

As is well known, every possible place has been assigned to this "feast" from the Passover of (say) 27 A.D. to the Feast of Purim of 28 A.D. In the extreme case of its being assigned to April A.D. 27, on the present arrangement of chapters in our New Testament we find an argument, begun at that date, resumed (VII 15 f.) and completed, with many cross-references, eighteen months later, in October 28. But not only is the argument so deferred, but the outbreak of hostility and deliberate plotting (V 16, 18) does not come to a head until the eighteen months have elapsed (VII 1). And when the narration of the plot is again taken up in VII 1 it stands out of connection, nothing in the preceding narrative as at present read (VI) supplying any link at all.

All these difficulties fall away, and cease to be, immediately we adopt the conclusions to which we have been led by the investigation of the narrative as it stands. Reading the history as originally arranged and now restored, we see how after spending the time of the Passover in Galilee (VI), Jesus went to Jerusalem at Pentecost, and then for the first time[1] meets with the threat of violence (V 16, 18). This

[1] In the narrative as now restored the definite outbreak of official hostility, it should be noted, falls within the last year of the ministry.

is met by massed arguments (19–47 + VII 15–19ᵃ), and then by Christ's calm unmasking of His enemies' intention: "Why are ye seeking to kill Me?" This quiet question thrills the people with amazement; incredulity is their mood at this time—an incredulity quite impossible in the present context, between the general fear of the "Jews" (13) and the public knowledge of the "Jews'" intention to kill (25), but quite in place in the month of May, when, at Pentecost, the first intimation of the settled policy of His enemies was made public. From Pentecost our rearranged narrative takes us to the Feast of Tabernacles (VII 2), and by this time, six months later, the intention of the priests is an open secret. Priests and multitude seek Him for different reasons; muttered questions (13) fill the streets with the atmosphere of assassination (25), and not only the streets, but the council chamber too, where Nicodemus, not vaguely perhaps, hints at illegal procedure (51). Thus the problem of the "feast" of V is solved, and the history of the year restored.

(2) But we also have removed for us a discrepancy that has seemed to mar the harmony of the Synoptic Gospels and the Fourth, or perhaps it will be more accurate to say that lines of agreement are now obvious that we could not trace before. Apart from the Passover of II 13 we have no visit of Jesus to Jerusalem recorded in the Fourth Gospel until the last year of His ministry, at Pentecost A.D. 28. This visit brings to a head the hostility of the "Jews," and this is followed by His return to Galilee. But, turning to the Synoptic narrative of the Galilean ministry, we

find that it was just at this time, viz. in the period following the Passover of 28 A.D., that Jesus (1) concluded His regular ministry in Galilee by (2) an irreparable breach with the Pharisees (Mk. VII). The narrative of John has already in VI shown us the widening breach between Jesus and the populace of Galilee (66). This is followed by what is practically a long-delayed declaration of war against the Pharisees by Jesus, for Mk. VII 1–23 can be looked upon as nothing less.

This double breach is again followed by journeys in various directions, to Jerusalem (Jn. V), to the borders of Tyre and Sidon (Mk. VII 24), to Dalmanutha (Mk. VIII 10), to the villages of Caesarea Philippi (Mk. VIII 27, Lk. IX 18 f.), and then, after fixed resolution to leave Galilee (Lk. IX 51) for Jerusalem, by journeys to that city, the first since Pentecost being recorded in John VII. The chapters VI, V, VII, as re-arranged, follow in train along the line of the Evangelic history from the crisis of the Galilean ministry to the outbreak of the undisguised hostility evoked by the ministry in Judaea. It therefore appears that the only argument against the entire compatibility of the narratives of Mark and John at this period of the ministry is the argument from the silence of Mark about journeys to Jerusalem—an argument not allowable in the case of so incomplete a narrative.

So far we have been indebted to Spitta only for
the transposition of VII 15–24, the reasons for adopt-
ing that transposition having been obtained by
independent investigation.   But, as we shall have in
the sequel to pursue our criticism of the text into
regions where Spitta has not entered, it will be well
at this point to give attention to his theory of the
disarrangement of passages.

He supposes that the misplacement of VII 15–24
and other paragraphs occurred through the leaves,
which had been pasted together, falling loose and
being put together in a wrong order, or through their
being first inscribed and then carelessly glued together in the order in which we now unfortunately
find them.   This means that the present result is due
to the disordering of chance.   This is unsatisfactory,
but, with the best will, I have been unable to find
any other cause, though in each particular case one
can detect some superficial reason for the present
connection.

The most interesting point, however, is that Spitta
has noted that each of the transposed passages is in
length, as nearly as possible, a multiple of the same
unit—that unit corresponding to the amount of writing probably contained in a single papyrus leaf[1].   It is
this " key " that is here adopted as a working hypothesis, and applied to other passages, some of them
not dealt with by Spitta.   The unit, or the multiple

---

[1] Spitta gives the length of VII 15–24 as 759 letters in Tischen-
dorf, and 778 in Tregelles, a difference of 19 letters.   I make it 14.

of the unit, is VII 15–24 = 18½ lines in W.H. small text. A passage to be considered later, XV–XVI, has 111–112 lines (allowing for gaps in type[1], etc.), and this is equal exactly to six units of the length of VII 15–24. This would be remarkable if it occurred in one case only, though not conclusive ; but we shall find similar results again and again. Applying the "key" to the long passage that we have found displaced without being broken up, viz. VI, we find on counting the lines, making careful allowance for spacings and differences of type, that it contains 130 lines, or a few letters over—that is, it contains seven pages of 18½ lines each. The fact that two lengthy passages answer so exactly to the test is no small confirmation of Spitta's theory that the displacements have been displacements of pages of equal size. But when we apply our measurements to V, which also comes into the question, since a bundle of pages (VI) has been moved from one end of it to the other, we find that it contains 84 lines—i.e., 4½ pages of 18½ lines each. This means, either that here Spitta's "key" does not answer, or that the unit is half of 18½, say 9·3 lines. We then have nine such pages in V. This measurement (9·3) we shall find receiving subsequent confirmation.

[1] On the other hand, in estimating the length of a passage, especially of a long passage, allowance must be made for the irregularity of ancient writing as compared with printing.

VII 53–VIII 11.

That this passage is an interpolation needs no
arguing.   But for this very reason it is all the more
interesting.   Omitted by all the great MSS. (except
D) it is a standing proof that the text of our Gospel
has suffered disruption.   At this part of chapters
VII–VIII our present text has undergone disarrangement.   Concerning this there is no doubt.   This
passage, therefore, affords a foothold, as it were, to
our investigation.

But this observation by no means exhausts the
interest attaching to the passage, for Spitta rightly
complains that the critics dismiss the paragraph without explaining its insertion at this point.   It is not
enough to omit it ; for, when it is omitted, it is found
that VII and VIII still do not dovetail.   Spitta
supposes that a blank space was left because of matter
lost.

This problem must be deferred until the following
paragraphs are under consideration.   Before we pass
on, however, it is to be noted that whether the paragraph, found first, among the Greek MSS., in Codex
Bezae, was inserted in a blank space, or displaced
another page found elsewhere, its length just fills our
hypothetic page or pages, being in its earlier and
shorter form (D) equal to 18 lines.

VIII 12–20.

When VII 53–VIII 11 is omitted, this paragraph (12–20) is brought into juxtaposition with VII, only to accentuate the difference of theme and situation[1]. The subject of the paragraph belongs elsewhere, as we shall see; and the situation is not that of departure as in VII 37 f., but of sustained argument. Moreover the statement of ver. 20 that "no man took Him, because His hour was not yet come" indicates a situation anterior even to VII 30 where the same statement is made, though its import implies a more advanced situation, as it follows on the statement that "they sought to take Him." Still more decisive is the crisis of VII 32 where the Pharisees sent officers to arrest Him. This, at any rate, is subsequent to VIII 20.

But the fact of the dissonance between VIII 12–20 and the end of VII needs not to be further argued, as it is generally allowed. Our task is to mark misplacement, and, if possible, effect restoration.

I cannot accept Spitta's treatment of this question. To say that VIII 12 has nothing to do with the

---

[1] "It is quite clear that this word αὐτοῖς (VIII 12) cannot mean either the members or the servants of the Sanhedrin, with whom the preceding notice is concerned." Wendt, *St John's Gospel*, p. 93.

Feast of Tabernacles is to go beyond the facts, though it may be that there is no *necessary* connection. Nor can I agree that the scene and argument of VII are closed in verses 47–52. The solution of Spitta, too, that a blank space was left because of matter lost, is too facile, and does not take in all the evidence.

As is indicated in the footnote just quoted from Wendt, this scholar has perceived the dislocation of the text, but his proffered restoration is not convincing. To say that VIII 12 "is a reiteration of VII 37–38" is only evidence of the misuse of words. To affirm that the connection of a saying concerning the Light of the World with a saying concerning the Water of Life is so necessary and immediate as to demand that all the intervening text be omitted so as to bring them into collocation—this is only to show that the thesis set forth is destitute of proof. Moreover, when Wendt writes: "These words in VIII 14 'I know whence I came, and whither I go' are a repetition of VII 28," he again misuses a word ("repetition"), and, more seriously, he fails to note that whereas in VII 28 the subject of origin (departure is not mentioned) is primary, in VIII 14 it is entirely subsidiary to the idea of witness-bearing (verses 14ᵃ, 15–18). This point is dealt with below. The connection of VIII 21 with VII, marked by Wendt, is made below, though in quite a different manner.

The solution of the difficulty lies in the removal of 12–20 from its present position; and this has a twofold bearing on the text.

(1) Examined by itself, this paragraph at once presents itself as the continuation and completion

of the already partially restored chapter V + VII
15–24.

(*a*) Omitting, as we may do without violence,
the opening words of ver. 12 (which are to be regarded
as a link inserted for the purpose of attaching a stray
paragraph to the narrative), we gain a perfect
sequence of thought: VII 24: "Judge not according
to appearance, but judge righteous judgment."
(VIII 12): "I am the light of the world: he that
followeth Me shall not walk in the darkness, but shall
have the light of life."

(*b*) VIII 13 f., concerning witness-bearing, refers
back to VII 16 f. and more remarkably still to V 31 f.
There is here what seems to be an apparent contradiction: "If I bear witness of Myself, My witness is
not true" (V 31). "Even if I bear witness of Myself,
My witness is true" (VIII 14). But in reality this is
an advance in Christ's argument during the Feast of
Pentecost. In the earlier part of the argument He
appeals to the witness of John, whom He speaks of,
it must be noted, as a lamp; and then to the witness
of His works, the witness of the Father (32–37).
Then Christ advances to the position that His
opponents are blinded to the true light by darkness
and perversion of mind (42–44). Yet if any man of
sincere heart desired to know, he might know (VII
17). Their judgment was that of the perverted
heart (VII 19–24)—they had not done even the
bidding of the light they had. The next step in the
argument is necessary, inevitable: in the face of
critics blind to the light through the essential false-
hood of their life and profession, Jesus steps forward:

" I am Myself *the* Light, and light is *self-evidencing* ;
even if I bear witness of Myself, My witness is true ;
it is the self-evidence of the Light" (VIII 12–14).
Witness of Father (V 37) and witness of Son (VIII
14) are one (18). In the present state of the text,
this argument is entirely lost.

(*c*) VIII 15 ("Ye judge after the flesh ") takes up
the immediately preceding VII 24, "Judge not
according to appearance."

(*d*) VIII 16 takes up again the thought of V 30
—the Son's judgment proceeds from the Father.

(*e*) VIII 18 ("The Father that sent Me")= V 37ᵃ.

(*f*) VIII 19 (ignorance of the Father)= V
37ᵇ–38.

The first result of this removal of VIII 12–20
from its present position and its restoration to its
original context is seen in the completion of chapter V,
which in its full extent is now seen to be V + VII
15–24 + VIII 12–20. This we may, for the sake of
brevity, refer to as " E " (fifth letter).

(2) The second result will be seen in the next
section (VIII 21–59).

Before passing on to that, we have to note that
the phenomenon of VII 53–VIII 11 does not stand
alone: the adjacent paragraph found in all the codices
is, like some others, misplaced. When measured,
this passage, 12–20, with the omission of the inserted
link πάλιν οὖν...λέγων, is found to be in length 18½
lines, exactly our unit (or multiple thereof). We find
then two passages of the same length inserted between
VII 52 and VIII 21.

A suggestion may be hazarded as to the reason

that led to the insertion of 12–20 immediately before
VIII 21, once it had gone astray. There is a resem-
blance, superficial only, between ver. 14 "ye know not
whence I come, or whither I go," and ver. 21 " I go
away." This would form an opportune link of
attachment. This perhaps confirms Spitta's verdict
concerning the twin paragraph VII 15–24 that it was
placed in its present position by the scribe of the
" liber nondum conglutinatus." The only reason
apparent for the insertion of this latter passage in
VII lies in an association of ideas between the teaching of Jesus (14) and its wonted result, "marvelling"
(15). In similar manner Zahn, *Introduction to New
Testament*, III, 346, accounts for the present position
of VII 53–VIII 11. Coming from Papias, Zahn
thinks it was inserted between VII 24 [subsequently,
of course, to the insertion of VII 15–24 in its present
position] and VIII 15, two sayings of Jesus about
true judgment. " This location would be also
favoured by the fine contrast between this passage
and the illegal proceedings of the session of the
Sanhedrin in VII 45–52."

VIII 21–59.

This passage is now, by the removal not only of VII 53–VIII 11, but also of VIII 12–20, brought into juxtaposition with VII, and we can now (1) rebut Spitta's charge that in dismissing the famous pericope no consideration of the remaining context is given, and (2) can decide whether there was a gap between VII and VIII.

The answer is that there was no gap, and that Spitta's difficulty is resolved by the removal of 12–20. For we find now that 21–59 follows on well after VII 52, completing the account of what took place at the Feast of the Tabernacles.

Ver. 21 well resumes after the discussion as to Christ's origin in VII 41 f., and 52 (last verse), and it also directly takes up the argument that preceded in VII 34 f., and so we find that, in sequence,

Ver. 22 answers to VII 35 ("whither will this man go?").

Ver. 26 answers to VII 28 ("He that sent Me is true").

Ver. 30 gives the same situation, or the development of the same situation ("many believed in Him") as is found in VII 31.

Accordingly we have chapter " F "

VII 1–14, 25–52 + VIII 21–59.

The hostility that we have traced in " E," and in its outbreak into publicity in the earlier part of " F," developes in the later part rapidly. The atmosphere suggests violence (22); twice Jesus tells them that He is aware of their murderous intention (37, 40); the end comes with an attempt to stone Him. Jesus escapes and does not re-appear in Jerusalem until the Feast of Dedication (IX–X), when another attempt is made upon Him (X 39).

The subject-matter of this restored chapter " F " is congruous. On the arrival of Jesus at the Temple (14) the subject of His origin is on the lips of the people. This Jesus takes up (28 f.), and it developes into that of His departure. The double subject remains the matter of public discussion (35 f., 41–52). In the following paragraph Jesus resumes it (VIII 21) with the people (22), and carries it to ultimate meanings (23–30). This is followed by the final paragraph (31–59), which is occupied with the diverse origins of Jesus and His opponents, and the results thereof as seen in their respective relations and bearings to the truth: " I speak the things which I have seen with My Father—ye do the things which ye heard from your father" (38). The diversity of attitude to the truth is explained by the diversity of the sources from which He and they draw their life and the inspirations of life.

Note on XII.

Though it is not the purpose of this Essay to register negative conclusions, Wendt's suggestion that the latter part of XII is disarranged is on the surface so similar to those made here, that at least a note of assent or dissent may be looked for. It must be one of dissent. To delete 36[b]–43, and connect 44 f. with 35–36[a] is at first sight obviously right. But it is only a mechanical jointure. If these verses stood alone, 44 would seem to belong to 35–36. But they do not ; they are parts of larger passages. And it is not possible to connect the tone of 44–50—a summary, as always understood—with the intense feeling of the most dramatic scene (20–36) in the Gospel.

II and III.

Our investigation must now be carried further, and our method applied to a passage that has hitherto escaped challenge—III 22–30.

This paragraph cuts into two what was originally one passage, the remaining sections of III.

That is, verses 31–36 should follow ver. 21 without any break.

(1) Against this is the apparently obvious reference in ver. 31 ("He that cometh from above...he that is of the earth...he that cometh from Heaven") to John the Baptist, whose words are found immediately preceding in 27–30.

But this easily assumed reference must be challenged and denied—it is a reference entirely due to the false context created by the displacement.

I would submit that the phrase ὁ ὢν ἐκ τῆς γῆς is not a phrase that the Evangelist would apply to the Forerunner. It is a phrase not found elsewhere in the Johannine writings in this sense (Westcott), but the whole verse must for purposes of interpretation be placed by the side of VIII 23 (ὑμεῖς ἐκ τῶν κάτω ἐστέ, ἐγὼ ἐκ τῶν ἄνω εἰμί· ὑμεῖς ἐκ τοῦ κόσμου τούτου ἐστέ). Without confusing the two words "earth" and "world," we are not transgressing the bounds of legitimate inference if we draw the conclusion that ὁ ὢν ἐκ τῆς γῆς κ.τ.λ. refers, not to the Forerunner but to those who "mind earthly things," who are on a lower plane of spiritual discernment where—for this is the burden of the whole chapter—faith in Christ (33, 36) is not possible.

The expression then in ver. 31 cannot be taken to refer to the Forerunner, and there is nothing else in 31–36 that can possibly be referred to the Baptist particularly. The conclusion, then, is that ver. 31 has been dissevered from its immediate connection : there is no kinship between 31–36 and 22–30.

(2)   The context in which 31–36 originally stood is found when 22–30 is deleted. We then have III in its true form, and it is at once seen that 31–36 supplies the completion of the Evangelist's comment (13–21) on the conversation between Christ and Nicodemus (1–12) :—

(*a*)   31 takes up the thought of 13—almost the *ipsissima verba*.

(*b*)   32 goes further back, and almost repeats the closing words of Jesus in the conversation (11). This shows that 31–36 is not an appendage to 22–30, but has reference only to the interview with Nicodemus.

(*c*)   34ᵃ (" He Whom God hath sent ") = 17ᵃ (" God sent...the Son into the world ").

(*d*)   The Father's love of the Son, whence comes the Son's critical position in the salvation of men (35), is the truth underlying the Son's mission and the salvation found in Him and Him alone (16–18).

(*e*)   36ᵃ—Faith leads to eternal life—this is the theme of 15–16.

(*f*) Finally in 36ᵇ (ὄψεται) there is a subtle but unmistakable link between the end of the chapter and the beginning in 3 (ἰδεῖν). Only those *within* the Kingdom can " see."

It is incredible that in the midst of so closely woven a passage there should have originally lain a paragraph telling of a geographical change of scene in the ministry, and an account of the ministry of John. (*a*) and (*b*) alone are enough to rule this out. So far then the conclusion is that III is restored to its original form, consecutiveness and unity, by the omission of 22–30.

(3) The disruption of context hereby revealed is perhaps the most striking example of the serious injury inflicted upon the text of the Fourth Gospel by the disarrangement of its leaves, and it raises the question how far the Gospel can be critically studied until its original order is approximately restored. This is a question not due for discussion here, our task being the attempt to restore the Gospel to its true order ; but we must, even at the risk of some slight repetition, mark even more clearly the solidarity and continuity of the dissevered sections.

The report of the interview between Christ and Nicodemus (1–12) is followed by two sections which are either reports of the further conversation rendered in and through the Evangelist's thought and word, or direct developments by the Evangelist himself. And it has to be noted that the second section (31–36), at present dissevered, is as closely, if not more closely, related to the conversation than the first (13–21). Moreover, as we have seen, the two sections are

themselves intimately related. This can be better
seen in the form of parallels :—

He that cometh from above is above all (31).	Thou art a teacher come from God (2). He that descended out of heaven (13).
He that is of the earth...of the earth he speaketh (31).	Except a man be born from above, he cannot see the Kingdom of God (3).
He that is of the earth is of the earth (31).	That which was born of the flesh is flesh (6).
What he hath seen and heard, of that he beareth witness (32).	We speak that we do know, and bear witness of that we have seen (11).
He that hath received his witness (33).	Ye receive not our witness (11).
He hath set his seal to this, that God is true (33).	How shall ye believe if I tell you heavenly things? (12).
He whom God hath sent (34) speaketh the words of God (34).	God...gave His only begotten Son (16). Whosoever believeth on Him ... hath ... eternal life (16).
The Father loveth the Son, and hath given all things into His hand (35).	God sent...the Son [His only begotten Son (16)] ... that the world should be saved through Him (18).
He that believeth on the Son hath eternal life (36).	Whosoever believeth in Him should have eternal life (16). He that believeth on Him is not judged (18).
He that obeyeth not the Son shall not see life, etc. (36).	He that believeth not hath been judged already, etc. (18).

It will be seen that, on the one hand, all the
leading thoughts of the conversation with Nicodemus
are taken up in 31–36, and on the other, all the words
of 31–36 are echoed from the conversation or its

development (1–18). Our conclusion then is confirmed, that 22–30, like VII 15–24 and VIII 12–20, is a foreign wedge driven into a wrong context. When it is removed, III is restored to unity and consecutiveness. The chapter has a conclusion (31–36) which, freed from its false attachment to the preceding account of the Baptist's ministry, is seen to be a complete summary, containing all the thoughts of the conversation of Jesus with Nicodemus.

(4) The paragraph 22–30, adrift from its first position, became attached to 31 because of the misinterpretation of 31 exposed above. The expression "from heaven" in 27 offered a sufficient link with the same expression in 31.

(5) The original position of the misplaced paragraph (22–30) was between verses 12 and 13 of II.

I would point out :—

(a) That the lack of transition between 12 and 13 in II is not after the manner of the Evangelist. The passing of Jesus from Galilee to Judaea is always noted, as is that from Judaea to Galilee. Here it is not. After a journey from Judaea to Galilee elaborately described (I 43–II 11) Jesus settles in Capernaum with His family (II 12)—and almost immediately we find Him going, not into Judaea, but directly to Jerusalem. We miss the usual phrase, covering an interval, "after these things." As the narrative stands, Jesus was back in Jerusalem three or four weeks after leaving Judaea. This can scarcely have been.

(b) On the other hand, where it stands, III 22 is not easy. The passing of Jesus into Judaea is

carefully noted, whereas in the context now preceding
He is already in Jerusalem—not, as we expect, in
Galilee. So not only does 22–30 dissect the context,
as we have seen in (2), but it also brings Jesus into
Judaea in words that imply a geographical situation
that is not found in the text now preceding.

These objections to II 13 and III 22 are both
removed if we place our paragraph 22–30 thus :—

> II 12.   In Capernaum.
>
> III 22–30.   To Judaea ; ministry there of some
>   duration.
>
> II 13 f.   *During this ministry in Judaea*
>   Passover at Jerusalem.

[It must not be inferred that the journey to Judaea
III 22ª, *immediately* followed the departure from
Capernaum (II 12 fin.). The words "after these
things" (III 22ª) cover an interval of some weeks or
months—they are so used in this Gospel, and here
they take the narrative over a period of the Galilean
ministry starting from Capernaum.]

We note the incidental gain that, by this re-
arrangement, the words of John (III 27–30), wherein
he refers to past utterances of his own, are brought
contextually much nearer to those utterances in I.
This only tends to confirm the conclusion that the
paragraph 22–30 is astray from its own context when
found in III, where it is only a wedge driven into the
unity of that chapter.

Moreover the chronological note (24)—"John was
not yet cast into prison"—is less of a difficulty the
earlier we can place it. The statement "not yet"
falls chronologically, it will be seen, in March 27—

this being the date of the passage in the following reconstruction, A.D. 29 being taken as the year of the Crucifixion.

(6) We can now garner the second result of our investigation in the field of the chronology of the Life of Christ.

The chief error in the accepted chronologies has been the placing of the Passover of II 13 at the very beginning of the ministry.

Obviously this beginning is too abrupt ; it contradicts too seriously the positive[1] tradition behind the Synoptic Gospels that the public[2] ministry opened spaciously, at some length, in Galilee—a tradition rendered unassailable by Acts X 37. This passage gives us the order :—

1. The baptism of John.

2. The Gospel—" beginning from Galilee."

3. " Published throughout all Judaea."

This is all in order with the evidence of the Synoptics conjoined with the Fourth Gospel as re-arranged.

There are three Passovers : II 13, VI 4, XVIII. These fall at the *end* of the three years respectively.

And leading up to the first Passover we have :—

(*a*) The return from the Temptation and the gathering of the first disciples, Jn. I 35 f.

---

[1] This is quite a different thing from the Fourth Gospel's contradiction of the Synoptists' silence ("negative" tradition) concerning journeys to Jerusalem which their later narrative implies.

[2] This does not militate against the historicity of the account in John I of the first personal attachment of disciples to Jesus. The difficulties of that passage fall outside the scope of this Essay, but they seem to be met most satisfactorily on the line of the suggestion in *Cambridge Biblical Essays* (ed. H. B. Swete, D.D.), pp. 306, 307.

(*b*)   A Galilean ministry, opened in Cana, Jn. II
1–11,

(*c*)   Carried on and gradually developed in and
from Capernaum Jn. II 12—after a stay in Capernaum
(Mk. I 21–34) of "not many days" (Mk. I 35, Jn. II 12),
taking in the surrounding towns and villages (Mk. I
38–II 17).

(*d*)   After a considerable interval thus occupied
("after these things"—a phrase always in John de-
noting such an interval), there follows a Judaean
ministry of early development, gaining converts and
arousing opposition—Jn. III 22–30 and, I think,
Mk. II 18–III 6.   These paragraphs in Mark
smack of Judaea and the controversies of Jerusalem.
Moreover, they are followed by a return to Galilee—
"Jesus with His disciples withdrew to the sea," followed,
be it noted, by a great multitude, not only of Galilee,
but from Jerusalem, Idumaea and beyond Jordan
(Mk. III 7–8).   This implies a ministry that had
already covered all the provinces of the land, and
that in no cursory fashion.

(*e*)   A Galilean ministry has then been followed
by a ministry in Judaea. In the midst of this Judaean
ministry fell the visit to Jerusalem for the Passover
(II 13–III).   Probably this visit occurred in the
earlier part of the sojourn in Judaea, and the ministry
there (III 22–30) continued afterwards even as far as,
it may be, November—December, if we so interpret
the "four months" of IV 35.   In the narrative the
Passover ministry in Jerusalem occupies far the larger
space (II 13–III 1–21, 31–36), but the shorter
narrative III 22–30 covers a larger tract of time,

including the former. "He tarried there" (22). Through the summer and possibly far into the autumn the ministry and the baptizing continued, extending so widely that the region "beyond Jordan" was affected, Idumaea heard the report thereof, and the Pharisees became alarmed ; whereupon Jesus left Judaea for Galilee (Jn. IV 1–3, Mk. III 7–8).

(f) Thus we get :—

(α) Opening ministry in Galilee. A.D. 26— March 27. Jn. II 1–12, Mk. I 38– II 17.

(β) Ministry in Jerusalem and Judaea. March 27—autumn 27. Jn. III 22–30, II 13– III, Mk. II 18–III 6.

(γ) Return to Galilee—Jn. IV, Mk. III 7–8.

(δ) Galilean ministry leading up to and beyond the Passover of A.D. 28. Jn. VI, Mk. III 7–VI et seq.

The remainder of the ministry has been already traced.

Our study of this part of the Gospel results, therefore, in the correction of misinterpretation, in the restoration of contexts, and in the simplification of the chronology of the life of Christ.

Now that we have quite independently arrived at our results with regard to this passage, it will be interesting again to apply Spitta's suggestion to a passage that has not come within his survey. We have found reason to regard 9·3 W.H. lines as the page unit. With its 17 lines III 22–30 barely fills two pages. Of course our measurement (9·3) is but

a rough estimate, and any inaccuracy or any irregularity in the manuscript in question would tell more
in a short passage than in a longer one. But we
have also to measure the larger space extending from
II 13 to III 21. Doing so, we find 65 lines—exactly
seven pages. This seems to me a remarkable confirmation of Spitta's theory, being, as it is, entirely
independent, and by him unsuspected. No single
passage would have any but the slightest weight ; but
the evidence is essentially cumulative.

XIII–XVII.

The disarrangement of these chapters is so widely acknowledged that our task will lie for the chief part in finding the true re-arrangement. XV–XVI are out of position after XIV, and some place anterior to XIV needs to be found for them.

(1) The reasons for disturbing the text as it now stands may however be briefly given.

(i) Not only is the last clause of XIV (" Arise, let us go hence ") indicative of conclusion to the conversation, and so unlikely to be followed by the larger part of that conversation (XV–XVI), but the same applies to the final paragraph of XIV as a whole (25–31). Here Jesus is taking His farewell in quite definite words. This is true indeed, of the whole chapter, but in 25–31 the chapter comes to its own natural conclusion. Jesus recalls His words just spoken as those of a time ("while yet abiding with you") now passing away. His place as teacher is about to be taken by the Paraclete (26). He makes His parting bequest—Peace (27)—before setting out on His journey to the Father (28–29). This journey opens immediately with an encounter that will take all His attention—an encounter so dread that He will have no time or word for His disciples during

its continuance, and, indeed, so dread that only at
His Father's express command does He enter into it
(30–31).

It is obviously impossible after this to think
of His entering on the long and, for the earlier
part of it, calm discourse contained in XV–XVI.
Remove these chapters, and there only remains XVII,
a prayer offered standing, containing no words, as
Spitta remarks, addressed to the disciples.

Spitta rightly rejects the well-known views that
XV–XVI were spoken standing, or that they are
an interpolation, or again a parallel account to
XIII–XIV.

(ii) Moreover, in XVI 5 we hear Christ say:
" None of you asketh Me ' Whither goest Thou ? ' "
This is startling after the long passage of statement
and question in XIII 36–XIV 5. And in XVI 17,
Spitta has well pointed out, the whispered questions
of the disciples show that they do not yet understand
about " Departure." It is only in XVI 29, after what
at the moment seems to them the clear statement of
ver. 28 (" I came out from the Father...I go unto
the Father ") that they get beyond their whispered
conference, and break silence.

(iii) As it stands, XIV should be followed by
an immediate or almost immediate change of scene.
This involves the leaving of the upper room, the
long continued conversation outside, and that too
after Jesus had declared He could speak no more
with them ; and, perhaps as great a difficulty as any,
the offering of the prayer outside the room.

We have already ruled out the second supposition.

It may be added that no change of scene is indicated until XVIII 1, and that there is no place for the prayer outside the upper room (Spitta).

It is only needed that we remove XV–XVI from their present position, and all becomes in order. Jesus brings His discourse to a close (XIV 25–31), offers prayer standing (XVII) and leaves the room (XVIII 1).

(iv) Before we seek the precise re-arrangement of the chapters, the thesis set forth may be put to preliminary test : how stands it with regard to the first references to the Paraclete in XIV and XV? Which of them is prior? The passages in question are :—

" When the Paraclete is come Whom I will send unto you from the Father, the Spirit of Truth, which proceedeth from the Father, He shall bear witness of Me " (XV 26).

" I will pray the Father, and He shall give you another Paraclete, that He may be with you for ever, the Spirit of Truth...for He abideth with you, and shall be in you " (XIV 16–17).

The two statements were spoken, it seems to me where there is little but impressions to guide us, in order as above, XV 26 being the earlier :—

(*a*) The statement in XV 26 seems to be a statement formally introductory of a Person hitherto unknown.

(*b*) The statement in XIV 16–17 is itself part of Christ's farewell. He is now filling the gap that will be left on His departure. The Paraclete has become His substitute and almost His Alter Ego.

He is to abide after Jesus has gone. So this passage in itself indicates that Jesus is drawing to the end of His discourse.

(c) It is important to note that the words "He abideth with you, and shall be in you" (XIV 17) would be incomprehensible to the disciples if spoken before those in XV 1–8, where "abiding" is explicated. Jesus could not have spoken of His Substitute abiding with them and in them before He had made clear the idea of His own abiding in them and theirs in Him as branches and vine.

We conclude then that the first reference to the Paraclete is found in XV 26, and this confirms the thesis already found to be probable.

This is again confirmed by the consideration of XVI 16, 22 and XIV 2. "A little while and ye behold Me no more...ye therefore now have sorrow : but I will see you again, and your heart shall rejoice, and your joy no one taketh away from you." These words, found in XVI 16, 22 are manifestly earlier, spoken from a position of narrower horizon, than those in XIV 1–3: "Let not your heart be troubled... In My Father's house are many abiding-places...I go to prepare a place for you. And if I go...I come again and will receive you unto Myself; that where I am, there ye may be also."

(2) In seeking the exact point from which XV–XVI have fallen out and to which they must be restored, we may start from the previous consideration of the posteriority of XIV 1–3, and thereby we are at once led to seek for the true position somewhere in XIII.

We may at once reject B. W. Bacon's[1] solution of the question : to place the chapters between verses 20 and 21 lands us in the impossible situation of having Judas in the room while the discourse on Friendship (XV—especially 13–17) proceeds! What are we to say about this kind of criticism ?

Not so preposterous, but almost as strange,. is Wendt's[2] contention that XV–XVI originally stood between verses 35 and 36. This suggestion is very strange because, in seeking to preserve a not very obviously necessary continuity between the record of the feet-washing and the exhortation to love one another (34), Wendt completely disrupts the passage 33–37 which is made a solid unity by its underlying subject—the departure of Jesus.

Leaving Bacon and Wendt, we may for a time follow the guidance of Spitta, who points out what has already independently been noted above, that XV 15 must have followed the departure of Judas—i.e. XV must follow after XIII 30. This is strengthened by the preliminary consideration that XV 15, 20 point to XIII 16, and are accordingly at least subsequent to XIII 20. The same inference follows from the comparison of XV 16 with XIII 18 (" I know whom I have chosen "). For these reasons we are led to the conclusion that XV–XVI fell originally not only after ver. 20, but after ver. 30, i.e. between ver. 30 and the beginning of XIV (see above).

The solution of the difficulty cannot be considered a satisfactory one which does not find a living con-

[1] *Journal of the Society for Biblical Literature*, 1894, pp. 64 ff.
[2] *The Gospel according to St John*, pp. 103 f.

nection between XIII and the allegory of the Vine
in the opening part of XV. This Spitta has found
by showing that the allegory of the Vine in part
refers to the "excision" of Judas. He rightly rejects
the usually suggested "occasions" for introducing the
figure of the vine, finding sufficient occasion in the
use of the fruit of the vine at the meal[1]. And with
what seems to me true exegetical insight, he connects
XV 2 ("every branch in Me that beareth not fruit, He
taketh it away[2]") with the departure—the "excision"
of Judas. Moreover, "ye are clean, but not all" in
XIII 10 before the departure of the traitor, becomes,
after it, in XV 3, "Already ye are clean" without
any exception.

Accordingly Spitta places XV–XVI after XIII
31ª—after the words λέγει 'Ιησοῦς, obtaining the
order: XIII 1–31ª, XV, XVI, XIII 31ᵇ–XIV, XVII.

This may, I think, be characterized as a brilliant
reconstruction of the text, and it is one that long
commended itself to my judgment. But I am forced
to dissent, and that for a reason precisely the reverse
of one that formerly led me to accept the position.
That reason, for which, among others, I accepted
Spitta's solution, was that it relieved us of that *crux
interpretum*, XIII 31.

This verse, linking the departure of Judas with
the "glory" of the Son of Man seemed incomprehensible (" When therefore he was gone out, Jesus

[1] Spitta's suggestion that an account of the Lord's Supper has
dropped out or been left out here does not materially affect the discussion.

[2] Cf. XV 6: "If a man abide not in Me, he is cast forth as a
branch...."

saith 'Now is the Son of Man glorified, and God is glorified in Him '"). No commentator had explained this, the apparently inexplicable; and it was because Spitta, by placing XV–XVI after λέγει Ἰησοῦς, had removed this difficulty, that his solution was all the more acceptable.

And it is just because further study of the Gospels has made clear the connection between the departure of Judas and the "glory" of the Son of Man and of God, that I am compelled to dissent from Spitta, and then to seek another solution, which, while conserving the integrity of ver. 31, retains all that Spitta has gained for us in this place.

(3) This involves an examination of the meaning in this part of the Gospel of the word "glory."

In chapters XI–XIII, which take us from the sickness of Lazarus to the departure of Judas, there is a frequent and remarkable recurrence of the idea of the glory of God, and this as an idea central and urgent in the mind of Jesus. And in His prayer (XVII) it is the one dominant thought.

It may be that I have been unfortunate, but research has failed to yield an adequate explanation of this word δόξα as used by Jesus. [The best I have seen is Principal Whitham's in Hastings' *Dictionary of Christ and the Gospels*.] For the most part commentators assume that the meaning of "glory" is self-evident; whereas in XII 43 ("they loved the glory of men more than the glory of God") John warns us that there is a glory of God that is not as the glory of men.

It is in this distinction between the glory that is after the heart of God and the glory that is after the

3—5

heart of man that we find the secret of these chapters
and of the life of Christ.

What then is the content, the peculiar content, of
the idea as it was in the mind of Jesus?

The key of interpretation is found in XII 20 ff.
The hour of the glory of the Son of Man had struck;
the Greeks were knocking at the door, and He was
ready in Himself; something of the possibilities,
something of what might have been, filled the thought
of Jesus; if only Israel had realised her mission, the
hour had come when she could have fulfilled her
calling and given to the world the Man for whom
the world in its heart was craving (21). But though
the hour had struck (23) Israel was not ready, and it
could not be. The Spirit of the Master is swayed to
and fro amid the tragedy of it all (24–27). All His
heart goes out to the world, but Israel stands between.
Then through the darkness and the regret strikes the
truth that there is another glory, a glory of God, a
glory not of earth, to which the Son of Man must
be raised, making real and manifest His Divine Son-
ship, the hourly and constant task of His earthly life.
The prayer "Save Me from this hour" is lost in the
prayer "Father, glorify Thy name" (27–28). From
the path that was His right (23) He turns to the path
opened by the Father—the path of sacrifice, which
is now revealed as the path of the glory of God.
This accepted, the heavens open, and Christ is once
more crowned, as at the sacrifice by the Jordan, and
on Mount Hermon[1], with the wreath of the praise of
God. This world is judged; its praise discarded;

[1] See my *Jesus, Son of God* (Elliot Stock), pp. 30 ff.

its prince cast out (31); its measurements and valua-
tions rejected; its glory passed, and the true light
from above is now among men (35). The glory of
God is sacrifice, the life of Love Divine.

We have now to see how this key thus gained, fits
other locks, and how it unlocks one never opened
before. We shall find that this meaning of the glory
of God, the revelation of sacrifice beyond the measure
of the thoughts of earth, the breath of Love that is
from above, runs through the chapters that are under
our consideration in which the Fourth Evangelist
brings to a climax his portraiture of Christ.

In XI 4 Jesus says that the sickness of Lazarus is
" for the glory of God," "that the Son of God [not
Son of Man] may be glorified thereby." It is alto-
gether unworthy to interpret this to mean that
Lazarus was to die in order that he might be raised
from the dead.

The thought of Jesus is revealed when we look at
the words in their historic position. The atmosphere
is one of peril, extreme, well-nigh hopeless, nay, quite
hopeless, Thomas thinks (16). It is only at the risk
of His life that Jesus can go to the help of His friends.
He goes, and He dies for it (XI 46, 53, XII 10
"Lazarus *also*"). The glory is seen in sacrifice.
" Greater love hath no man than this, that a man lay
down his life for his friends" (XV 13).

What now is the meaning of our passage XIII 31 ?
"When therefore he [Judas] was gone out, Jesus
saith : ' Now [at last] is the Son of Man glorified and
God is glorified in Him.'" The Son of Man has
reached the glory of God.

It is admitted that this is a *crux interpretum*. So impossible seems any connection between the dismissal of Judas (Christ's failure?) and the glory of God, that Spitta finds here, as we have seen, the place to insert XV–XVI.

Again the historic situation gives us the light. By careful arrangement Jesus had secured the upper room in an unknown situation, unknown even to the Apostles until they were guided thither. In order to guard His privacy for a few hours He must take Judas with Him, and keep him for as long as possible in the room so that he cannot tell the priests. But the hour comes when the presence of Judas is no longer possible; the circle of friends must be free from the traitor[1]. But how get him out of the room alive?

John tells us that no man knew why he went out. It was superbly managed. But for that masterly care, the sword of Peter would have been in the traitor's heart, and Barabbas would have hung on the central cross on the morrow. Jesus saved Judas at the cost of His own life.

The Son of Man had achieved the glory of God—sacrifice.

Finally, right through the prayer of XVII Jesus is praying for the endowment of Calvary. The supreme sacrifice had been made in the Heart of God before the world was (XVII 5, cf. Rev. XIII 8). That He might in the flesh and through death unite Himself in this with the Father was His deepest prayer (XVII 24).

---

[1] For this reason it is impossible to insert XV–XVI after XIII 20 as some do. These chapters were not spoken with Judas in the room.

I would submit then that it is not admissible to disrupt XIII 31—that the verse has a meaning very wonderful, but strictly in accord with the thought growing to a climax through the foregoing chapters: that when Jesus had saved Judas and got him out of the room alive and unsuspected, the glory of God was realised in the Son of Man by sacrifice, by that love, like no other, that can follow, even unto death and sacrifice, the hardened heart: sacrifice and love to be completely revealed (32) on Calvary.

(4) It remains to find the place where XV–XVI may be inserted, the place from which they have been displaced.

This I find between verses 32 and 33—i.e. immediately after the passage we have been considering.

There is an obvious gap between 32 and 33. The arrangement of paragraphs here in R.V. and W.H. has long seemed to me faulty.

On the one hand, it is only the common interpretation given to "glory" that seems to afford a link between 32 and 33—the idea of ascension. That removed, there is none.

On the other hand (a) 31–32 obviously reads as the conclusion of a foregoing narrative, and we need either a new subject, or, as we shall find, a discourse (XV) immediately springing out of the foregoing situation. (b) ver. 33 is really what we may call the beginning of XIV.

Thus our arrangement is :—

XIII 1–32.
XV–XVI.
XIII 33–XIV.
XVII.

This arrangement retains all the felicities of Spitta's, and removes all the difficulties of order and situation. All the original difficulties as to the questions of the Apostles and the position of XIV are dispelled, and we gain the to me irresistible conjunction of the dismissal of Judas with the words of Jesus about the branch that is "cast forth" (XV 2,6)—these words being Christ's spoken thoughts arising out of the situation as He knew it to be.

The connection between XIII 1–32 and the opening of XV–XVI being thus re-woven, the record proceeds without disruption through the two chapters, and it remains for us to make clear that at the other end there is no ill-woven connection. There is no difficulty here. At the end of XVI Jesus takes up again what He had darkly hinted at earlier in the evening (16), viz. the subject of His departure (28). This being made definite, He leaves them the bequest of His Peace (33). So we naturally, without any break or jolt, pass, in the re-arranged text, to XIII 33 : "Little children, yet a little while I am with you. Ye shall seek Me...whither I go ye cannot come"—words that open the closing section of the evening's record, that of farewell and the opening unto them of the Eternal Abode of God's Peace (XIII 33–XIV).

So not only do we find connection restored between XIII 1–32 and the beginning of XV–XVI, but we also have restored to us that between the end of XV–XVI and XIII 33 ff. The connections, hitherto severed, stand clearly out.

Spitta has acutely pointed out that :—

(i)   Jn. XVI 32 ("ye shall be scattered, etc.") is the equivalent of Matt. XVI 31 (= Mk. XIV 27)—

" I will smite the shepherd and the sheep...shall be scattered " ;

(ii) This declaration in both Matt. and Mark precedes the announcement of the denial of our Lord by Peter ;

(iii) This same declaration precedes the same announcement in the Fourth Gospel as now re-arranged.

As before observed XV–XVI contain 111–112 lines, equal exactly to 12 pages of 9·3 lines each (W.H.).

(5) We may now review the re-arranged chapters as a whole, to mark the progress of thought and the order of its unfolding. The chapters are commanded by the introductory words of XIII 1 :—

(a) Jesus knew that the hour of His departure had come. This is the thought at the back of His words all through the evening, but naturally it will come to the front last of all, and only after He has led up to it the prepared hearts of His friends. This we find to be so in the primitive order of the record, now restored.

(b) Jesus had spent His life in love of " His own which were in the world."

(c) This love He now carries to its completeness.

(i) The first movements revealed in the records are the steps taken by Jesus to make those that are " His own " more than ever His own, His own in spirit, in tone and temper of mind and intent of heart, and to purge that circle of any who will not so accord. This is accomplished by the ordeal of the feet-washing, and the white light of His own spirit and mind of utter humility and devotion therein revealed. This effects (a) the cleansing of the hearts of those that loved Him, the toning and ordering of their spirits for what is to follow; and (β) the excision of the recalcitrant Judas, this utterly painful and tragic event being brought about, not by the swift denouncing and destruction of the traitor, but by the sacrifice of His own safety—in other words by the sovereignty of that spirit of devotion even to the unworthy and of the sacrifice of self which is the very glory of God and which was to be the redeeming power in that upper room and for ever afterwards beyond its walls. Thus far XIII 2–32.

(ii) Jesus now immediately (XV 1 ff.) unfolds the meaning of this accomplished fact which we have divined in the record as His initial purpose. The unfruitful branch has been removed, and the fruitful branches made clean by the inspiration of His "word," the "word" that bore the burden of His innermost spirit.

(iii) The way is now clear for the revelation of Love. The Vine's life is now revealed, allegory apart, to be the Life of Love. XIII 1 is now explicated. He who has "loved His own which were in the world" can speak to understanding hearts of that love (XV 9 ff.), and of that love becoming a new life in them, so that, living one life, Master and disciples may be for ever united in an eternal fellowship. Thus He follows up the cleansing of their hearts by the inspiration of His own innermost life.

(iv) But this fellowship lights up the dark background of the world's hate against which it will have to be maintained. But even this is transfigured by fellowship of fortune with Himself. And these sentences (XV 18 ff.) become an application in general to the Apostles and the world of the truth as to essential opposition just made clear between Jesus and Judas. This essential opposition will make necessary the work of the Advocate Who will plead the cause of Jesus (26) after His departure, convict the world of its error and guilt, and perfect in the disciples the revelation of their Master (XVI 1–15).

(v) The thought of departure has slipped in, though not of death. Here the Master lingers, that the unwonted idea may find a lodgement in startled minds. [It may be noted how natural our revised order is as compared with the "Textus Receptus," wherein the clear declaration of XIII 33–XIV *precedes* the curious puzzlement of XVI 16 ff.] Leading them gently on, He is at length able to confront them with the hour of danger that will break upon them when they find themselves alone (32). Then He flings over them the shield of His Peace (33), under its guard speaking plainly of His departure, unaccompanied (XIII 33 f.), and of Simon Peter's denial. So sure is the guard, so firm the hand that holds it, that He can speak of their continued life of love which they shall lead in His name, spite of all and, again spite of all—departure through death, their loneliness and Simon's denial—can bid them be of heart untroubled (XIII 34–XIV 1).

The fitness of our re-arrangement is finally confirmed by the way, as seen above, in which in passing from XVI to XIII 33 f. we find the two thoughts of XVI, departure and peace, immediately taken up and completed, the other thought of XVI that of the Paraclete, being subsequently developed in XIV.

(vi) Over this chapter (XIV) we need not linger long. It unfolds itself now, in its true place, as the culmination of all that has gone before. The departure is lost in the light of Eternal fellowship in the Spirit. The Upper Room gives place to the Father's House. Jesus takes those He loves with Him. And when they stand to pray (XVII), it is beyond Calvary, beyond the grave, in the near Presence of the Father.

In conclusion, the re-arranged Gospel stands thus :—

$$I–II \ 12$$

$$\begin{cases} III \ 22–30 \\ II \ 13–III \ 21 + 31–36 \end{cases}$$

$$IV$$

VI

V + VII 15–24 + VIII 12–20

VII 1–14 + 25–52 + VIII 21–59

$$IX–XII$$

XIII 1–32

XV–XVI

XIII 33–XIV

$$XVII$$

$$XVIII–XX$$

$$XXI.$$

For EU product safety concerns, contact us at Calle de José Abascal, 56–1°, 28003 Madrid, Spain or eugpsr@cambridge.org.

www.ingramcontent.com/pod-product-compliance
Ingram Content Group UK Ltd.
Pitfield, Milton Keynes, MK11 3LW, UK
UKHW020312140625
459647UK00018B/1831